Quests for Gold

by Lillian Forman

Editorial Offices: Glenview, Illinois • Parsippany, New Jersey • New York, New York
Sales Offices: Needham, Massachusetts • Duluth, Georgia • Glenview, Illinois
Coppell, Texas • Ontario, California • Mesa, Arizona

Every effort has been made to secure permission and provide appropriate credit for photographic material. The publisher deeply regrets any omission and pledges to correct errors called to its attention in subsequent editions.

Unless otherwise acknowledged, all photographs are the property of Scott Foresman, a division of Pearson Education.

Photo locators denoted as follows: Top (T), Center (C), Bottom (B), Left (L), Right (R), Background (Bkgd)

Opener ©Carl & Ann Purcell/Corbis; 1 ©Vanni Archive/Corbis; 5 (L) ©Vanni Archive/ Corbis, 5 (R) ©Roger Wood/Corbis; 6 ©Elio Ciol/Corbis; 7 (T) ©Charles O'Rear/Corbis, 7 (C) ©Phil Schermeister/Corbis, 7 (B) ©Matthias Kulka/Corbis; 9 ©Historical Picture Archive/Corbis; 11 ©Carl & Ann Purcell/Corbis, 11 (BG) ©Historical Picture Archive/ Corbis; 12 ©Gianni Dagli Orti/Corbis; 13 Corbis; 14 Bettmann/Corbis; 16 ©Bettmann/ Corbis; 19 ©Stephen Frink/Corbis

ISBN: 0-328-13662-X

CONTENTS

Chapter 1

A Brief History of Gold

Long ago, explorers faced danger and hardship looking for legendary cities made of gold. During the California Gold Rush that started in 1848, miners worked day and night in hopes of finding inexhaustible sources of gold.

In many societies, great wealth was often passed on from one generation to the next. Nonetheless, there were always adventurers looking for gold.

Gold may be one of the first things that humans wanted but didn't need. Scientists have found small nuggets of gold in Spanish caves scattered among human bones and skulls that seem to date back to 40,000 B.C. When the owners of the gold died, their friends and relatives buried them with the bits of metal. It was the custom at that time to lay people to rest with their favorite things around them.

In ancient times, people had not yet invented the art of writing. Since they were unable to record their thoughts and feelings, it is impossible to know what gold meant to them. All we know is that they kept the metal without changing it in any way. They must have thought it had a value that did not depend on everyday use.

The oldest known pieces of gold jewelry date back to 3000 B.C. They were found in the tombs of Sumerian kings.

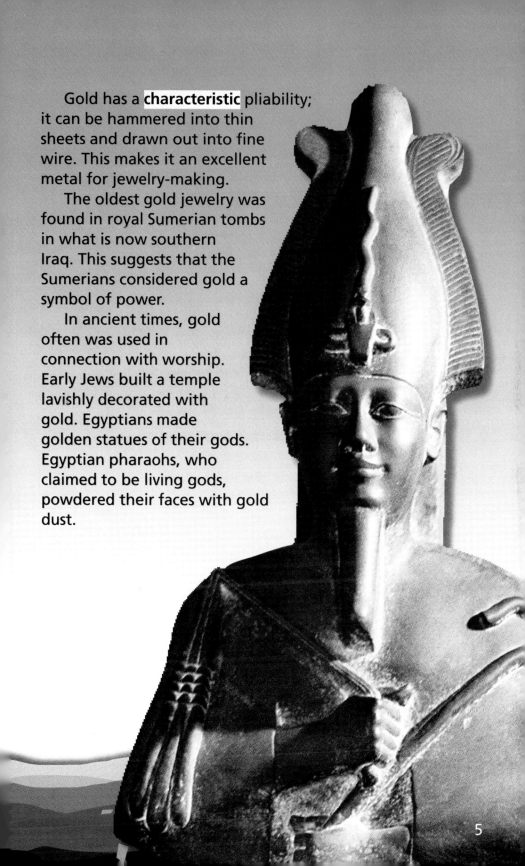

Gold has a **characteristic** pliability; it can be hammered into thin sheets and drawn out into fine wire. This makes it an excellent metal for jewelry-making.

The oldest gold jewelry was found in royal Sumerian tombs in what is now southern Iraq. This suggests that the Sumerians considered gold a symbol of power.

In ancient times, gold often was used in connection with worship. Early Jews built a temple lavishly decorated with gold. Egyptians made golden statues of their gods. Egyptian pharaohs, who claimed to be living gods, powdered their faces with gold dust.

Chapter 2

Gold as Money

Today we use gold for money. Our money system was once based on the value of gold. This system was called the gold standard. It meant money could be exchanged for a specific amount of gold. We do not use the gold standard today. The value of money changes from day to day. The time line shows important dates in the history of gold being used for money.

Ancient people paid for goods and services with cattle, slaves, and land. But by 4000 B.C., Egyptians used gold bars as payment. In 700 B.C., Lydians, in what is now the Middle East, traded golden coins for goods. These coins all shared the same weight and value.

The use of gold currency allowed common people to save money. Before gold money, people traded in goods, which could not be stored easily. Gold does not **corrode** so it could be saved to buy property.

Once money had the same value in Europe and in Asia, merchants could trade fairly.

4000 B.C.	The Egyptians use gold bars for money.
700 B.C.	The people of Lydia, in Asia Minor, make coins of pure gold that all have the same weight.
A.D. 1284	Venice begins using the ducat, which becomes the most widely used coin for more than five centuries.
1717	The Master of the London Mint sets a price for gold that remains in effect for more than 200 years.
1792	The United States defines the U.S. dollar as worth 24.75 grains of gold and 371.25 grains of silver.
1900	U.S. currency is placed on the gold standard.
1934	President Franklin D. Roosevelt sets the price of gold at $35 an ounce.
1944	The International Monetary Fund (IMF) and the World Bank are established.
1973	The U.S. dollar is taken off the gold standard.
1999	The European Union introduces the euro.

Chapter 3

Jason and the Golden Fleece

The story of "Jason and the Golden Fleece" may be only a myth, but myths continue to be told and enjoyed because they describe experiences and feelings that are common to many people. In this myth, the human desire for gold and power is explored.

Jason was the nephew of a Greek king, Pelias. The young man was well liked and had a strong claim to the throne, but Pelias decided to get rid of him. He promised to give Jason the kingdom if he would find the golden fleece of a magical ram. Pelias expected the fierce dragon that guarded the fleece to kill his troublesome nephew.

Jason set off with a group of friends to where the fleece was located. When they got there, Medea, the daughter of that country's king, fell in love with Jason. After Jason promised to marry her, Medea used a magical potion to put the dragon to sleep, and Jason grabbed the fleece. He then went on to deal with other dangers and pursue other accomplishments. However, the main idea of this myth is that gold has the power to both create and destroy a king.

9

Chapter 4

Gold in the Americas

When Christopher Columbus landed in the Caribbean in 1492 and claimed it for Spain, he believed that he had found a new trade route to Asia and access to its spices, silk, and gold. He believed that Spanish merchants could gain control over trade with India. When the Spaniards realized instead that they were in a position to acquire a vast continent, they were determined to **exploit** their opportunity.

Hernando Cortés came to Cuba in 1504 and was given land and slaves. But Cortés was not satisfied; he had come for gold. In 1519, he led a military expedition to Mexico to find it.

In Mexico, Cortés found what he had been looking for. The Aztecs mistook Cortés and his followers for gods. Aztec myths said that their god Quetzalcoatl would return at about the time that Cortés and his army arrived in Mexico. The Aztec ruler Moctezuma sent the Spaniards disks of silver and gold.

The Aztec craftspeople and artists created beautiful works of art. Some were made of gold and silver.

Southwest of
North America

Mexico

Cuba

Peru

New Spain 1500–1800

11

Tenochtitlan, capital of the Aztec Empire

These fabulous gifts doomed the Aztecs. Convinced now that he was about to discover vast treasure, Cortés planned his assault. His army had guns and horses. The Aztecs had neither. The Aztecs were harsh rulers and had many enemies. With the help of neighboring native peoples who hated the Aztecs, Cortés and his small army conquered the Aztec empire. The Spaniards tore down their capital city, Tenochtitlán, and built Mexico City on its foundation.

The Aztecs were an advanced civilization with an understanding of literature, science, and art. The conquering Spaniards destroyed the Aztecs' books and melted down their golden ornaments to make gold coins. The Spaniards enslaved the Aztecs and forced them to work in the mines.

Cortés and those who followed him ruled over Mexico with great cruelty. As they conquered other Mexican natives, such as the Maya, they destroyed their civilizations as well. Soon Mexico, now called New Spain, was like a factory that turned out gold and silver for Spain. The Spaniards justified their actions by saying that they would save the souls of those they conquered by converting them to Christianity.

Gold is rare because it is hard to find. Soon the Spaniards had managed to **extract** most of the gold from all the known mines in Mexico. The Spanish colonists tried to find other mines. They questioned the Native Americans and sent explorers into areas not yet settled by Spaniards.

Spanish explorer Francisco Pizarro

A **rumor** about a place in the Americas called El Dorado spread through New Spain. The Native Americans claimed that when the people of El Dorado chose a new chief, they covered him in gold dust. Then the chief gave his people emeralds. The Spanish seized on this idea and stepped up their explorations.

In the 1530s, Francisco Pizarro's search for El Dorado led him into South America. He did not find the city, but by tricking the Incan people, he conquered them and captured their wealth. He invited their ruler, whom the Incan people saw as a god, to meet with him. The ruler told his bodyguards to disarm in order to avoid offending the foreigners. Pizarro took the ruler prisoner and then had him killed.

Explorers continued to look for more gold to **hoard.** A new rumor spread about seven golden cities located in what is now the southwestern United States. A Spanish priest called Fray Marcos de Niza started this rumor, based on information he had received from Native Americans.

Fray Marcos persuaded a young Spaniard named Francisco Coronado to explore the region. Coronado found nothing but villages inhabited by peaceful farmers. In spite of the lack of gold, Coronado claimed the land for Spain, which controlled much of what is now the western United States until the early 1800s.

Francisco Coronado and his expedition

Chapter 5

The Gold Rush

One winter morning in 1848, a Californian named James Marshall was building a sawmill called Sutter's Mill. In the river near the mill, he saw a shiny object. When he picked it up, he felt convinced that it was gold. Marshall was right. His discovery started a headlong rush to California.

Many people headed west to find gold. The Forty-Niners, as they were called, were sure that they would gain a fortune. But few ever did. Most of the gold was found by the very first miners who arrived.

Not only did the goldfields yield only small amounts of gold to the Forty-Niners, but the large number of people who rushed to California also caused prices of goods to rise steeply. Aside from a few lucky miners, most of the Forty-Niners were shocked to discover that they were barely able to pay for their daily needs. Also, the work was hard. The miners had to spend long hours crouched in the water sifting sand and gravel to find a few grains of gold. Many returned home penniless.

The people who traveled to California in 1849 to find gold were called the Forty-Niners.

The miners who stayed in the goldfields could no longer find gold nuggets near the surface or by panning in streambeds. They began to work together and use other means to find gold on their claims.

At first, miners dammed rivers in order to change the course of the water. This exposed the original riverbed, giving the miners easier access to the gold at or just beneath the surface. Soon, though, they had extracted all the gold they could find in that way. Then a new technology came to the goldfields. This new mining method used the enormous power of water.

Miners began to channel the water of the rivers—and the energy it generated—into huge pipes. The pressure sent powerful jets of water out the other end of the pipes. Miners used the blasting water to strip away the riverbanks and riverbeds, sometimes to bedrock. Then they used machinery to separate the broken rocks and soil to find the gold.

The rivers and the environment surrounding them were almost entirely destroyed. Eventually, this method of mining was banned, but the damage was done.

Chapter 6

Gold Today

Gold is still being mined today in many nations around the globe. South Africa produces the most gold. It accounts for about one-third of the gold produced every year. Gold is also mined extensively in Russia, Australia, Canada, China, and the United States. The state of Nevada currently produces the most gold of any of the fifty states.

Today, in addition to its financial and decorative purposes, gold plays an important role in technology. Because gold conducts electricity well, it is used to plate electrical contacts and circuits, including those on computer circuit boards. The airbags in our cars use gold-plated contacts.

Because gold reflects heat rays so well, the exteriors of some satellites are fitted with thin golden film to help control temperatures in space. The visors on astronauts' space suits are also coated with this thin film of gold. Here on Earth, gold is mixed into window glass for use in high-rise buildings. The gold in the windows helps reflect the sun's heat and reduces air conditioning costs. These are only a few of the technological uses for gold.

Even today, gold can lead people into adventure. In September 2004, an article titled "Legendary City of El Dorado Exists" appeared in *Discovery News*. The article reported the finding of a document that describes Paititi, a city with gold-painted walls. According to this document, a priest found the city during the sixteenth century but kept its location a secret.

An adventurer named Jacek Palkiewiiz was certain that he could find the lost city. In 1996, he was able to locate the real source of the Amazon River. He claimed that he had already found the square lake and waterfall that mark the entrance to Paititi.

In addition, modern scuba divers sometimes search for treasure ships that were **engulfed** by the sea during storms long ago. Today, however, most explorers don't keep the treasure they find. They turn it over to museums and researchers to help people better understand history.

Historical events and the legend of Jason and the Golden Fleece show that gold can cast a spell over people. It can drive them to risk their own lives and to hurt others. Modern searches suggest that in addition to the desire for power and riches, people search for gold because they are curious and adventurous. From the beginning of the human race, such characteristics have led people to explore new regions of the world.

Glossary

characteristic *adj.* special; distinctive.

corrode *v.* to wear away gradually (usually by chemical action).

engulfed *v.* to have flowed over and enclosed.

exploit *v.* to use; to take advantage of.

extract *v.* to draw forth.

hoard *v.* to grab or store a large supply of something.